11/11

R

MILWAUKEE
BUCKS

by Gary Derong

Published by ABDO Publishing Company, 8000 West 78th Street, Edina, Minnesota 55439. Copyright © 2012 by Abdo Consulting Group, Inc. International copyrights reserved in all countries. No part of this book may be reproduced in any form without written permission from the publisher. SportsZone™ is a trademark and logo of ABDO Publishing Company.

Printed in the United States of America,
North Mankato, Minnesota
062011
092011

 THIS BOOK CONTAINS AT LEAST 10% RECYCLED MATERIALS.

Editors: Matt Tustison, Dave McMahon
Copy Editor: Anna Comstock
Series design: Christa Schneider
Cover production: Craig Hinton
Interior production: Carol Castro

Photo Credits: Lynne Sladky/AP Images, cover; Focus On Sport/Getty Images, 1, 42 (top); AP Images, 4, 8, 13, 14, 19, 25, 26, 31; Ron Koch/AP Images, 7, 42 (middle); Diamond Images/Getty Images, 10; Vernon Biever/NBAE/Getty Images, 17; Fred Jewell/AP Images, 20; Harold Filan/AP Images, 23; Ronald C. Modra/Getty Images, 28, 43 (top); Dick Raphael/NBAE/Getty Images, 33; Darren Hauck/AP Images, 34, 42 (bottom); Ezra Shaw/Getty Images, 37; Morry Gash/AP Images, 38, 43 (middle); Jeffrey Phelps/AP Images, 41, 43 (bottom); Darren Hauck/AP Images, 44; Gary Dineen/NBAE/Getty Images, 47

Library of Congress Cataloging-in-Publication Data
Derong, Gary, 1950-
  Milwaukee Bucks / by Gary Derong.
      p. cm. -- (Inside the NBA)
  Includes index.
  ISBN 978-1-61783-164-5
  1. Milwaukee Bucks (Basketball team)--History--Juvenile literature. I. Title.
  GV885.52.M54D47 2012
  796.323'640977595--dc22
                                   2011015973

TABLE OF CONTENTS

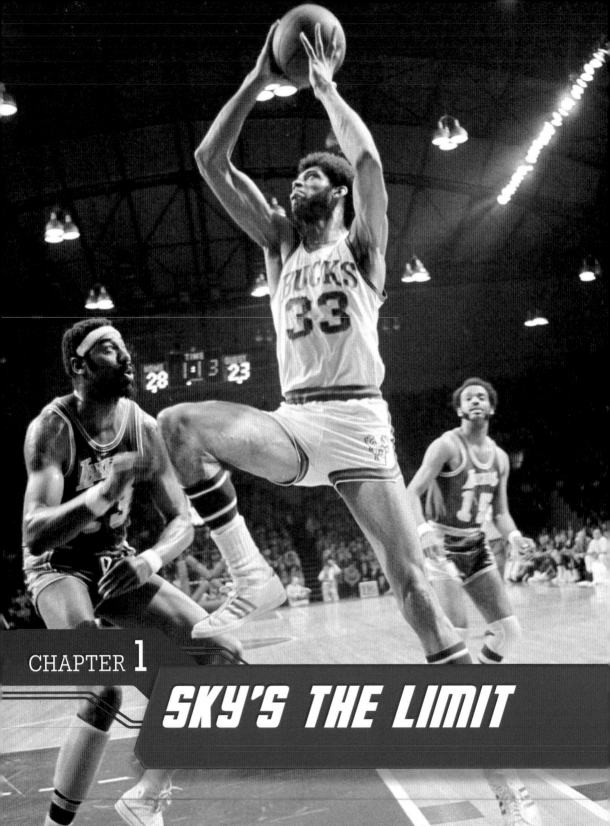

CHAPTER 1

SKY'S THE LIMIT

It was all coming so fast for Milwaukee's basketball fans. They had a National Basketball Association (NBA) expansion team one year. That team qualified for the playoffs the next year. And then this: "LEW ALCINDOR Milwaukee Dynasty."

The cover of the *Sporting News* on February 13, 1971, featured a full-page photo of Alcindor, the Milwaukee Bucks' 7-foot-2 center, and actually used the word "dynasty" in the headline. Could the baby Bucks be on the verge of a championship run that would last for years—maybe even decades?

The Bucks had not won anything yet. But if anyone could lead them on such a run, it was Alcindor. He had done that very thing for his high school and college teams. And his first season in the NBA had turned the Bucks from a group of castoffs into a playoff team. Alcindor was a fast, mobile giant on the court. His shot-blocking skills could scare anyone thinking about driving to the basket. Not only that, he

Bucks center Lew Alcindor goes up for a shot against the Lakers' Wilt Chamberlain in the 1971 playoffs. Alcindor led Milwaukee to the NBA title that year.

MILWAUKEE KNOW-HOW

The Bucks' quick rise to power was unique to the NBA but not to Milwaukee. The city's baseball team performed a similar trick during the 1950s.

Unlike the Bucks, the Milwaukee Braves were not an expansion team. They were a team that fell on hard times after playing in the 1948 World Series as the Boston Braves. The arrival of Ted Williams to Boston's other baseball team, the Red Sox, doomed the Braves to second-class status in Boston.

In 1953, the Braves' owner moved the team to Milwaukee. They went from a seventh-place team in 1952 to a second-place contender in the National League as Milwaukee's much-loved team. Hank Aaron arrived in 1954 to join Eddie Mathews, Warren Spahn, and Lew Burdette on a team that set attendance records and went on to win the World Series in 1957.

had a shot that could not be blocked: the skyhook.

Hook shots were from a bygone era. They typically looked like one-handed push shots and were not very glamorous. But Alcindor would fully raise his shooting arm to flick a one-hander *downward* at the 10-foot-high basket. A defender who swatted it away would be called for goaltending, and two points would go up on the scoreboard. Alcindor could shoot the skyhook with either hand, and from as far as 20 feet from the basket.

"Right now, there is nobody in the league who influences a game as much as Alcindor," New York Knicks center Willis Reed said in an article in that same February 13, 1971, *Sporting News*.

Reed was the reigning NBA Most Valuable Player (MVP). The Knicks were the

The Bucks' Oscar Robertson handles the ball against the Knicks in November 1970. Milwaukee's acquisition of Robertson helped the team dominate during the 1970–71 season.

defending NBA champions. In a memorable playoff series between the Knicks and the Bucks in April 1970, Reed had used every trick he knew to battle the much-taller Alcindor.

The Bucks learned in that series loss that they needed another star to compete for a title. And that player arrived in a trade the day after New York ended Milwaukee's

Hello to Big O

"*Oscar Robertson is without a doubt the greatest basketball player I have ever played against,*" said Jerry West, a fellow Hall of Famer who was so good that his likeness was used to create the NBA logo. In 10 seasons with the Cincinnati Royals, the Big O showed that he could do it all—except single-handedly win a championship. So he welcomed the trade to Milwaukee on April 21, 1970, and the opportunity to team with Lew Alcindor. "*I feel I will fit in there very nicely,*" he said.

Coach Larry Costello is surrounded by his starting five on the 1970–71 Bucks: *(clockwise from top left)*, Bob Dandridge, Lew Alcindor, Greg Smith, Oscar Robertson, and Jon McGlocklin.

1969–70 season. His name: Oscar Robertson.

Robertson was known as the "Big O." He was an ideal addition to a young Bucks team. Robertson was on the downside of his career. But he was very versatile. A point guard with good size, Robertson was a skilled passer, outside shooter, and rebounder. When defenders sagged around Alcindor, Robertson could make them pay by passing or shooting. He teamed with Jon McGlocklin to give the Bucks a strong backcourt.

Long-range shots were like rare gems in the NBA in those

days. The three-point shot existed only in the rival American Basketball Association (ABA). The focus of NBA teams was instead on getting high-percentage shots. And that is why the play of the league's centers was so important to their teams.

When Alcindor got stuck with the ball in a traffic jam of defenders, he would look to pass to forward Bob Dandridge. Dandridge was so skinny that his teammates called him "Pick." This was short for toothpick. He had a deadly soft touch on short jump shots and the ability to slice through a crowded lane for layups, putbacks, and rebounds.

Greg Smith, the man known as "Captain Marvel," was at the other forward position. Smith was not much of a scorer and was not very big at 6 feet 5 inches and 200 pounds.

The Taskmaster

The Bucks had the most creative center and point guard in the NBA, yet they ran more set plays than any team in the league. Larry Costello—the first coach in Bucks history—was a stickler for being prepared. "The plays don't always work, but I figure we've got a better chance at two points if everyone has something special to do," he said. Costello's ever-present notepad became a trademark.

But the scrappy Smith had powerful legs and little regard for his safety. The Milwaukee Arena crowd would roar in delight when he launched himself in pursuit of a loose ball.

"He's our spark, our life," Bucks coach Larry Costello said. "He has the knack of covering great distances and a sense of being in the place where the ball is."

Costello's starting five featured Dandridge, Smith, McGlocklin, Robertson, and

The Bucks' Lew Alcindor, *middle*, leaps high into the air to battle the Lakers' Happy Hairston, *left*, for a rebound in the 1971 Western Conference finals. Milwaukee won the series in five games.

Alcindor. Forward Bob Boozer and guard Lucius Allen were the first two off the bench. And in the 1970–71 season, playing in front of home crowds still new to the NBA, that group dominated the league.

Milwaukee won 20 straight games, an NBA record at the time, during a late-season drive. They captured the Midwest Division title with a 66–16 record. The Bucks had one of the greatest offensive teams in league history, with a scoring average of 118 points per game. And they were the first team in NBA history to make more shots than they missed.

Points were falling from the sky with Alcindor's sky-hook. Alcindor led the league in scoring that season with 31.7 points per game and was named MVP. Robertson dropped from a 30-point scorer with his former team, the Cincinnati Royals, to a 20-point player in his first season with the Bucks. Getting the ball to Alcindor was his first priority.

With their two superstars leading the way, the Bucks made quick work of their playoff opponents. Losing their home court, the Milwaukee Arena, did not even bother them. The arena was hosting other events. So the first round of the play-offs was moved 80 miles west to Madison, Wisconsin. The Bucks needed only five games to get the required four victories against the San Francisco Warriors. Their clinching win was a 50-point mauling on the University of Wisconsin's court.

A star-studded matchup with the Los Angeles Lakers in the Western Conference finals was next. But the Lakers were missing guard Jerry West and forward Elgin Baylor because of injuries. Aging center Wilt Chamberlain was left to carry the load for Los Angeles. Milwaukee cruised to the series victory once again by four games to one.

So there the Bucks were, in their first NBA Finals. And they had barely worked up a sweat. They were feeling fresh

Eye on the Knicks

The team that knocked the Bucks out of the playoffs in 1970 continued to give them problems the next season. The New York Knicks beat Milwaukee in four of their five meetings in the 1970–71 regular season. But the Bucks got lucky—twice. They were moved into the Western Conference while the Knicks stayed in the East. And the second break came when the Baltimore Bullets ousted the Knicks in the Eastern Conference final. That kept the Bucks from having to play them in the Finals.

and fired up to be playing the Baltimore Bullets for the title. The Bullets, on the other hand, were in bad shape. They had outlasted the New York Knicks in a grueling seven-game series. And their three stars—center Wes Unseld, guard Earl Monroe, and forward Gus Johnson—all were slowed by injuries.

The Bucks turned to their defense to smother the Bullets. With their best scorers limping around, the Bullets found Alcindor and his long arms to be menacing. "You've got to give Lew all the credit," Baltimore guard Kevin Loughery said. "He may just block one shot here or there, but guys have to change their shots because of him."

Milwaukee swept the Bullets in four games. It was only the second such sweep in NBA Finals history. Alcindor was named the Finals MVP, adding to his regular-season award. But the most appreciative Buck was the Big O. The 11-year veteran had never before won a title.

"This is the thrill to cap all thrills," Robertson said. "No matter how many individual records you set, the big thing is to win a title. Now I've finally got one."

Success came so fast and so easily for Milwaukee that the cover of the *Sporting News* actually seemed believable to fans: "LEW ALCINDOR Milwaukee Dynasty."

With teammate Oscar Robertson (1) setting a screen, the Bucks' Lucius Allen drives with the ball against the Bullets during the 1971 NBA Finals. Milwaukee swept Baltimore in four games.

CHAPTER 2

TAILS WE WIN

Milwaukee had an exciting, winning basketball team in the fall of 1968. But it was not the Bucks. The Marquette University Warriors were on the rise under coach Al McGuire. And there was rarely a dull moment around the team and its coach.

McGuire was a New Yorker. He was brash, colorful, stylish, and hot-tempered. The Milwaukee newspapers and TV stations gave him a lot of attention.

Then along came a new NBA team in the fall of 1968 to share the Milwaukee Arena with the Warriors. The owners of the new team wanted McGuire to be their coach. But Marquette would not let him out of his contract. That turned out to be a good move for the university. McGuire coached the Warriors until they won the National Collegiate Athletic Association (NCAA) championship in 1977.

Bucks coach Larry Costello shouts during a game against the Celtics in November 1968. Milwaukee finished its first NBA season 27–55.

MILWAUKEE HAWKS

Milwaukee got its first taste of NBA basketball when the Tri-Cities Blackhawks—later shortened to the Hawks—were moved to the newly built Milwaukee Arena for the 1951–52 season.

The team consistently finished last in its division. But a huge sign of hope arrived before the 1954–55 season when the Hawks drafted 6-foot-9 forward Bob Pettit. The talented big man had a spectacular rookie season, averaging 20.4 points per game and winning Rookie of the Year honors. But he could not prevent the Hawks from finishing last in the West for a fourth straight season.

By that time, Milwaukee sports fans were all wrapped up in their newest professional team. The Hawks could not compete with the baseball Braves for attention. So owner Ben Kerner moved the Hawks to St. Louis in 1955. They were then moved to Atlanta in 1968.

Because Milwaukee's NBA club was an expansion team, it had no big stars. Its roster was stocked with players who had been backups for other teams in the league. And after failing to land McGuire, the Bucks even got their coach from the expansion draft. Larry Costello was a guard for the Philadelphia 76ers who suffered leg problems that caused him to retire as a player. But he had shown an ability to coach. So the Bucks chose him in the player draft and then signed him as a coach.

The team's owners, Marvin Fishman and Wesley Pavalon, got a great basketball man named Ray Patterson to run the club as president. Fishman and Pavalon also hired University of Wisconsin coach John Erickson as general manager. Milwaukee

Bucks guard Jon McGlocklin tries to keep the ball away from a Bullets defender in the late 1960s. McGlocklin was an original member of the franchise.

found three quality players in the expansion draft: guard Jon McGlocklin, forward Bob Love, and center Wayne Embry. But the Bucks traded Love to the Chicago Bulls early in their first season and received guard Flynn Robinson.

The Bucks and the Bulls were natural rivals, as Chicago is situated 70 miles (112 km)

"Deer" to Their Hearts

The nickname "Bucks" came from a name-the-team contest. R. D. Trebilcox of Whitefish Bay, Wisconsin, was one of 45 people who suggested the name. His explanation—"Bucks are spirited, good jumpers, fast and agile"—won him a new car. Team management ended up choosing the second-most popular nickname. The most popular nickname was "Robins."

from Milwaukee. The rivalry started during Milwaukee's first regular-season game. The Bucks lost 89–84 in front of 8,467 fans at the Milwaukee Arena. The Bucks' first victory came in their sixth game, a 134–118 win over the visiting Detroit Pistons on Halloween night.

The Bucks went on to win 27 games that season. This total marked the second-most victories by an expansion team. But they finished last in the Eastern Division. Their last-place finish meant they would participate in a coin flip with their expansion mates, the Phoenix Suns, to determine which team would pick first in the 1969 NBA Draft.

The stakes were enormous. Winning the flip would bring a future superstar to the team. The Suns had won only 16 games in their first season. They received the right to call heads or tails. They called heads. NBA commissioner Walter Kennedy's coin came up tails.

Milwaukee had won the right to draft Lew Alcindor. He was the amazing center for coach John Wooden's national champion University of California, Los Angeles (UCLA) team. Before that, Alcindor had starred at New York City's Power Memorial Academy High School. Jubilation erupted in the Bucks' offices.

One obstacle still remained for the Bucks. The rival ABA had similar designs on Alcindor. And as a two-year-old

Former UCLA star Lew Alcindor signs a contract with the Bucks in April 1969. Milwaukee general manager John Erickson, *right*, and coach Larry Costello look on.

league, the ABA had more riding on signing him than did the NBA. Alcindor said he preferred to play professional ball in his hometown of New York. As luck would have it, the New York Nets wound up with the ABA's rights to him. Alcindor decided to accept one secret offer from each league. He said he would go with the highest offer.

The financial terms of the offers were never revealed. But the Bucks' five-year offer was believed to be worth $1.4 million and the Nets' five-year offer worth $1 million. Alcindor was true to his word and was in the lineup when Milwaukee opened the 1969–70 season against visiting Detroit.

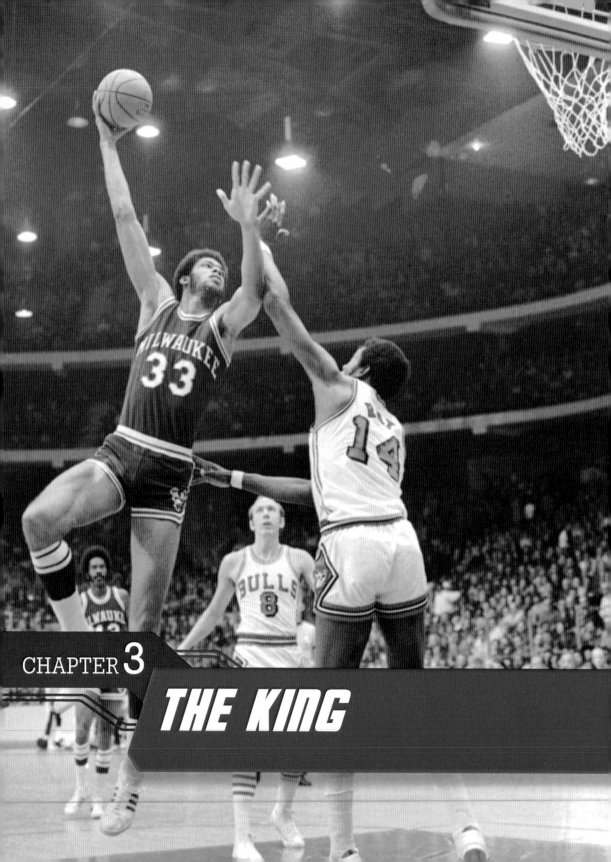

CHAPTER 3

THE KING

Bucks fans felt good about their NBA championship in 1971. But they were not sure how to feel about their new superstar.

The fans knew Lew Alcindor had grown up on one coast of the United States, attended college on the other coast, and was not very fond of the Midwest. They also knew that he guarded his privacy and did not reveal much about himself in interviews.

Before the 1971–72 season, the star center made it known that he no longer wanted to be called Lew Alcindor. He said he had changed his religious beliefs from Catholicism to Islam. He had taken the name Kareem Abdul-Jabbar, which means "noble, powerful servant." The name change made him even more of a mystery man in Milwaukee. But most fans figured if he was happy, they were

Bucks center Kareem Abdul-Jabbar, formerly known as Lew Alcindor, goes up for a skyhook against the Bulls in November 1971.

happy. They swapped their souvenir Alcindor shirts for ones that read "Abdul-Jabbar" above his No. 33.

"The people in Milwaukee were good about it. They realized I wasn't some sort of idiot," Abdul-Jabbar later recalled. "The coach, Larry Costello, had some trouble. He kept stumbling— 'Lew . . . Kareem . . . Lew . . . Kareem.' He was very self-conscious about not saying the wrong thing."

Untimely Turnover

Messing with a championship team is dangerous, and the Bucks paid a price for doing it after their 1970–71 title run. They lost team president Ray Patterson, the man who had built their title team. He left for a similar job with the Houston Rockets. They also lost "Captain Marvel" Greg Smith. Smith was traded to Houston for little-known forward Curtis Perry and a draft choice. The Bucks were not the same team without him.

To Bucks radio broadcaster Eddie Doucette, Abdul-Jabbar was simply "the King." And to the NBA, he was the MVP.

Abdul-Jabbar repeated as league scoring champion in 1971–72. He averaged 34.8 points per game. He was once again named the NBA's MVP. But the Bucks' championship run ended at one. They had an outstanding 63–19 regular season. One of the victories came in a midseason game that drew huge national attention. On a cold January day in 1972, a sellout crowd at the Milwaukee Arena watched the Bucks end the Los Angeles Lakers' record 33-game winning streak with a 120–104 victory. Abdul-Jabbar had 39 points. Jerry West led Los Angeles with just 20.

But the Lakers finished with a better regular-season record, 69–13, than the Bucks. And they knocked Milwaukee

The Bucks' Kareem Abdul-Jabbar, *left*, and Curtis Perry battle the Lakers' Wilt Chamberlain for the ball in the 1972 Western Conference finals. Los Angeles ousted defending champion Milwaukee in six games.

out of the playoffs by winning four of the six games played in the Western Conference finals.

The Bucks went 60–22 the next season. But they suffered a first-round playoff loss to the Golden State Warriors. Then in 1973–74 came a 59–23 season. Abdul-Jabbar captured his third league MVP honor. And Milwaukee earned a fourth straight division title and went on a whale of a playoff run.

The Bucks opened the 1974 playoffs by eliminating the Lakers in five games. And after sweeping the Chicago Bulls in four, they were headed to the

Calling Dr. J

The Bucks used a first-round draft choice in 1972 to select Julius Erving, nicknamed "Dr. J," who then was playing for the Virginia Squires of the ABA. They took a chance that the forward might want to play with a great center like Kareem Abdul-Jabbar. But he ended up staying on the East Coast and continued his standout play for the Squires and, later, the New York Nets. When the ABA folded in 1976 and a handful of teams moved to the NBA, Erving left the Nets and was sold to the Philadelphia 76ers. He starred with them for many years.

NBA Finals against the Boston Celtics. Abdul-Jabbar gave Milwaukee an edge up front. But Boston had a very strong backcourt. The Bucks' Oscar Robertson was slowing with age. Also, the team's quickest guard, Lucius Allen, was out of the playoffs with an injury.

Boston used a full-court press to thoroughly rattle Milwaukee's guards in Game 1. The visiting Celtics won 98–83.

The host Bucks captured Game 2 105–96 in overtime. But Game 3 was another case of Boston's press causing bad passes and turnovers. The host Celtics won that one 95–83.

Coach Larry Costello made a lineup change that helped the Bucks even the series with a 97–89 road win in Game 4. But that lineup change left Robertson as the only guard on the floor for Milwaukee. His energy was being used up just bringing the ball up the court against Boston's press, led by Jo Jo White.

Not even Abdul-Jabbar's 37 points and 11 rebounds could save the Bucks from a 96–87 home loss in Game 5. They went to Boston knowing one more loss would end their season.

Game 6 became one of the closest games in NBA playoff history. Regulation time ended with the score tied at 86–86.

Milwaukee star Kareem Abdul-Jabbar accepts the league's regular-season MVP Award before Game 1 of the 1974 NBA Finals.

Just before the first five-minute overtime ended, Boston's John Havlicek followed his own missed shot with a put-back to make it 90–90.

In the second overtime, Havlicek struck again when he arched a 15-foot jump shot just over Abdul-Jabbar's outstretched hand to put the Celtics up 101–100. Only seven seconds were left. The Bucks called a timeout and designed a play for Jon McGlocklin, their long-range shooter.

McGlocklin was guarded, so Robertson lofted a pass to Abdul-Jabbar. The big center had a defender draped all over him when he unleashed

Kareem Abdul-Jabbar lets go what would be the winning shot in Milwaukee's double-overtime victory at Boston in Game 6 of the 1974 NBA Finals.

a skyhook from the baseline. It dropped through with three seconds left. The Bucks held on to win 102–101 and tie the series.

The excitement of Game 7 in Milwaukee did not last long. The Bucks' backcourt was ailing and exhausted. The Celtics gave center Dave Cowens enough help to contain Abdul-Jabbar in a 102–87, title-clinching victory for Boston.

Robertson announced his retirement following the season. As the supporting cast for Abdul-Jabbar weakened, his anger surfaced more often.

After suffering his second serious eye injury in a 1974 exhibition game, he slammed a basket support in anger and broke his hand. And with their star on the injured list to start the season, the Bucks won only three of their first 16 games. They finished that injury-riddled season with a 38–44 record and missed the playoffs.

After that season, the Bucks gave their unhappy superstar a change of scenery. They traded Abdul-Jabbar and center Walt Wesley to the Lakers for center Elmore Smith, guard Brian Winters, forward David Meyers, and forward/guard Junior Bridgeman.

The team that once had people dreaming of a dynasty would have a devil of a time even making it back to the NBA Finals without the King.

KID STUFF

Kareem Abdul-Jabbar said he practiced his hook shot a lot when he started playing basketball in fourth grade.

"It was the only shot I could shoot that didn't get smashed back in my face," he said. "So I learned to rely on it early, and it was always something that I could get off, even in traffic."

Because the NCAA had banned the dunk when Abdul-Jabbar was in college, he used the hook to help UCLA win 88 of the 90 games in which he played. His ability to shoot the hook downward to the basket inspired Bucks broadcaster Eddie Doucette to give it the name "skyhook." And Abdul-Jabbar shot it with such accuracy that he averaged 30.4 points per game with a shooting percentage of 55 percent during his time with the Bucks.

CHAPTER **4**

NELLIE'S TEAM

The Bucks were changing on and off the court after the trade of Kareem Abdul-Jabbar to the Los Angeles Lakers in June 1975.

Guard Jon McGlocklin retired after the 1975–76 season. He was the last of the original Bucks players. Not long after that, the team was sold to Jim Fitzgerald, a cable television executive. Larry Costello, the only coach in team history, resigned after a 3–15 start to the 1976–77 season. Replacing Costello was a young coach with no experience. Thankfully for the Bucks, Don Nelson was a quick learner.

Nelson was a former bench player for the Boston Celtics. He endured a last-place finish in his first season as Milwaukee's coach. But he led the rebuilding Bucks to a second-place finish and first-round playoff series victory over the Phoenix Suns in 1978. Nelson, nicknamed "Nellie," gave the team stability

Don Nelson, shown in 1978, had no head coaching experience when he went from being a Bucks assistant to head coach in late 1976. But he would be successful, as he guided Milwaukee for 11 seasons.

OPENING NIGHT SHOCK

The 1977–78 season opener featured the most shocking moment in Bucks history.

The Bucks were unveiling a brand new center, Kent Benson, whom they selected number one overall in the 1977 NBA Draft. And Benson was making his debut against none other than Kareem Abdul-Jabbar and the Los Angeles Lakers.

A mere two minutes into the game in Milwaukee, Abdul-Jabbar punched Benson in the face for what Abdul-Jabbar believed was an overly aggressive elbow Benson planted in the superstar's chest. The brutal punch broke Benson's jaw and gave him a concussion. Abdul-Jabbar broke his hand and missed 20 games because of the injury. The NBA fined him $5,000, and he was widely criticized in the media. Benson, a former Indiana University star, never lived up to his promise as an NBA player after that start.

and became a fan favorite during his 11 seasons as coach. He was named NBA Coach of the Year twice in that time.

"Nellie" was hurting for a dominant center. So in 1980 the Bucks acquired Bob Lanier from the Detroit Pistons. Lanier was not Abdul-Jabbar. But he was a future Hall of Famer. The Bucks won 20 of their last 26 games in 1980 after acquiring Lanier. And that got fans excited about what he and the team could do in a full season.

The Bucks made it all the way back to 60 wins in 1980–81. That was their first season in the Eastern Conference's Central Division. Lanier averaged only 14 points. But he was a polished veteran who played good defense and made his teammates better. The best of those teammates were guards Sidney Moncrief

The Bucks' Bob Lanier, *left*, and Marques Johnson double team the 76ers' Julius Erving during a 1981 playoff series. Philadelphia won the series in seven games.

and Quinn Buckner, forward Marques Johnson, and guard/forward Junior Bridgeman.

As good as the Bucks were, they could not get past a star-laden Philadelphia 76ers team in the playoffs. The Sixers knocked them out again in 1982 and 1983. The Bucks got one more season out of Lanier and reached the Eastern Conference

Flashy Floor

The Milwaukee Arena went from a plain-looking building with an ordinary name to the MECCA Arena in 1974. MECCA stood for Milwaukee Exposition and Convention Center and Arena. In 1977, the arena received a colorful, artistic basketball floor that prominently featured the letter "M" and delighted television viewers. Pop artist Robert Indiana added to his fame by designing the floor.

finals in 1984 before bowing to the Boston Celtics in five games.

Milwaukee then traded Johnson, Bridgeman, and center-forward Harvey Catchings to the Los Angeles Clippers for forward Terry Cummings and guards Ricky Pierce and Craig Hodges. It was up to Cummings and Moncrief to carry the scoring load. And they did, as the Bucks won two more Central Division titles in 1986–87.

"Nellie"

Don Nelson not only was the best coach in Bucks history. He also had the most victories of any coach in NBA history through the 2010–11 season, with a career record of 1,335–1,063. After coaching the Bucks from 1976 to 1987, Nelson went on to coach several other clubs. As the Bucks' coach and player personnel director, he built a team that won seven straight division titles from 1980 to 1986. Milwaukee led the league in fewest points allowed in 1983–84 and 1984–85.

The Bucks entered the 1986–87 season with a new, veteran center. Jack Sikma was acquired in a trade with the Seattle SuperSonics. Sikma averaged a solid 12.7 points and 10 rebounds that season. And Milwaukee already had several other solid scorers in Cummings, Moncrief, forward Paul Pressey, and guards Pierce and Hodges. The team was so balanced that seven Bucks averaged in double figures. Cummings led the way at 20.8 points per game. Milwaukee also had the player considered as the league's top reserve in Pierce. He won the Sixth Man Award with his ability to come off the bench and light up the scoreboard.

But the most important Bucks player let them down that season—Sidney Moncrief, a 6-foot-4, 190-pound guard. A consistent 20-point scorer,

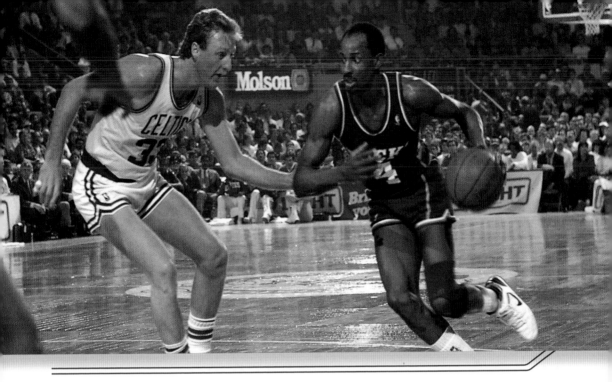

The Bucks' Sidney Moncrief drives against the Celtics' Larry Bird during the teams' 1987 second-round playoff series. Boston won in seven games.

Moncrief was twice named the NBA's Defensive Player of the Year. He was a five-time All-Star. But in 1986–87, the season the Bucks appeared ready to win the Eastern Conference title, Moncrief broke down. He missed 43 games with foot and knee problems. When he did play, he averaged only 11.8 points.

Moncrief's return near the end of the season helped the Bucks survive a tough five-game playoff series against the 76ers. And they took the mighty Celtics to seven games before being ousted in the Eastern Conference semifinals. But Moncrief would be reduced to playing a smaller role on future Bucks teams. And he would be doing it for a new coach.

BUMPY RIDE

T

he Bucks changed coaches, owners, and arenas in the mid- to late-1980s. They also nearly changed cities.

The MECCA, with a seating capacity of 11,052, had become the smallest arena in the NBA. In 1985, Jim Fitzgerald and his ownership partners decided to sell the team. Minneapolis-St. Paul, with no NBA team at the time, had a group willing to buy the Bucks and move them to Minnesota. But up stepped Herb Kohl. Kohl was a Milwaukee businessman who had just sold his interest in the Kohl's department store chain. He bought the Bucks for $18 million because he said he wanted to keep them in Wisconsin.

Kohl was not as rich as most of the other NBA owners. So the Bucks could not spend a lot of money on players. But he received a wonderful gift after he bought the team: a new arena. A wealthy couple named Lloyd and Jane Pettit said they would build a new arena for

Herb Kohl, shown in 2003, bought the Bucks from Jim Fitzgerald in 1985 to make sure that the team stayed in Milwaukee.

THE SENATOR

Herb Kohl and his family ran a chain of grocery and department stores that still carries their name. His name is on the University of Wisconsin's Kohl Center arena because his $25 million donation helped construct it.

He kept the Bucks in Milwaukee at least twice by buying the team in 1985 amid interest from a Minneapolis–St. Paul group, and by saying no to Michael Jordan. The former Chicago Bulls superstar asked Kohl in 2008 to sell him the team but was turned down.

Kohl, who began serving as a United States senator in 1988, enjoys both of his roles in Wisconsin.

"A senator's job is more important in terms of representing our state, people's hopes and dreams, and the lives of their children. . . . But I love owning the team," Kohl said. "It's one of the happiest experiences of my life."

Milwaukee and give it Jane's family name. The Bradley Center would house the minor league hockey team the Pettits owned, as well as the Bucks and Marquette University's basketball teams.

The 20,000-seat Bradley Center opened on October 1, 1988. It was hoped that the larger crowds the Bucks could draw would help the team earn enough money to join the NBA's elite teams. But new ownership and a new arena could not make up for the loss of coach Don Nelson. Nelson had such a great relationship with Fitzgerald that he followed the former Bucks owner out of town. Nelson left after the 1986–87 season to coach the Golden State Warriors—the team that Fitzgerald bought.

A Bucks team that had had only two coaches in its

Left to right, Ray Allen, Glenn Robinson, Sam Cassell, and Tim Thomas react during the Bucks' Game 7 loss to the 76ers in the 2001 Eastern Conference finals.

history suddenly got used to making a coaching change every few years.

The 1990s were a horrible decade for Bucks basketball. A bench player, Ricky Pierce, was the team's leading scorer for the 1989–90 season. That season, Milwaukee set a team record for the number of games missed by players because of injuries. Even so, that 1989–90 team managed the only play-off game victory in the entire decade. The Bucks went seven straight years without making the playoffs. And the worst record in Bucks history, 20–62, was compiled in the 1993–94 season.

A return to respectability started on August 29, 1998,

The Bucks' Andrew Bogut drives against the Trail Blazers' Joel Przybilla in December 2006. Bogut gave Milwaukee a strong inside presence.

with the hiring of George Karl as the club's seventh coach. The Bucks immediately became a playoff team under Karl. He had been a successful coach with the Seattle SuperSonics. In 2000–01, the Bucks won the Central Division with a 52–30 record and made it to the Eastern Conference finals. Guards Ray Allen and Sam Cassell, and forward Glenn Robinson led the way. However, old rivals, the Philadelphia 76ers, ousted the Bucks in seven games. Allen Iverson scored 44 points for Philadelphia in its 108–91 home win in Game 7.

Injuries, age, and the lack of a dominant center prevented

Karl from ever achieving an NBA title in Milwaukee. He and the Bucks parted ways after the 2002–03 season.

The center the Bucks had been lacking arrived with the number one overall draft choice in 2005. Versatile 7-foot Andrew Bogut was selected. The native Australian had played college ball at the University of Utah.

Bogut became a more reliable scorer, rebounder, defender, and shot-blocker. But he also showed that he needed more help. After the Bucks slumped to three straight fifth-place finishes in the Central Division, Kohl responded. He put a new man in charge of his basketball operation.

John Hammond had helped build the Detroit Pistons into a championship team. The Bucks hired him as general manager on April 11, 2008. Ten days later, Hammond introduced a new coach, Scott Skiles. Skiles had eight years of NBA coaching experience and was known for stressing defense and gritty play.

Under Skiles, the Bucks would be less of a jump-shooting team and more of a fast-breaking team that looked for layups. They would be more exciting to watch. They also would put their offense in the hands of a rookie point guard who did not even have college experience.

All-Time Team

The Bucks celebrated their fortieth anniversary in 2008 by naming a 20-member all-time team. Fans voted online, and here is who they chose in alphabetical order: Kareem Abdul-Jabbar, Ray Allen, Vin Baker, Junior Bridgeman, Quinn Buckner, Sam Cassell, Terry Cummings, Bob Dandridge, Marques Johnson, Bob Lanier, Jon McGlocklin, Sidney Moncrief, Ricky Pierce, Paul Pressey, Michael Redd, Alvin Robertson, Oscar Robertson, Glenn Robinson, Jack Sikma, and Brian Winters.

Scoring Mark Falls

Rookie Brandon Jennings scored 55 points in only his seventh NBA game—Milwaukee's 129–125 victory over visiting Golden State on November 14, 2009. That broke Kareem Abdul-Jabbar's team rookie record of 51 points and came within two points of matching Michael Redd's team record of 57. Warriors coach Don Nelson called Jennings's outing "probably the best rookie performance I've ever witnessed in 30-some years of coaching."

The Bucks used the 10th pick in the 2009 NBA Draft to select guard Brandon Jennings. He was the national high school player of the year as a senior at Oak Hill Academy in Virginia. But he left the United States after that to play profession-ally in Italy. After one year overseas, Jennings entered the NBA Draft. He was somewhat of a mystery to league scouts because he was only a year removed from high school and had been out of sight for a year.

However, Hammond was confident that Jennings had the makings of an NBA star. So he drafted him. And Jen-nings made the Bucks' general manager look good right away. Jennings scored 17 points, had nine assists, and grabbed nine rebounds in Milwaukee's 2009–10 season opener at Phil-adelphia. The Bucks lost 99–86. But the 20-year-old youngster showed he could be a big-time scorer, crash the boards, and direct an up-tempo offense.

Bucks fans were excited. But Hammond had more work to do. Longtime scoring star Michael Redd suffered one major knee injury after another and was lost for the season in January 2010. It is not easy to find a good shooting guard at midseason. But Hammond managed to land veteran John Salmons from the Chicago Bulls in February.

Rookie Brandon Jennings celebrates during Milwaukee's 129–125 home win over Golden State in November 2009. Jennings scored 55 points.

Salmons proved to be a great fit. The Bucks finished second in the Central Division with a rookie point guard and without Redd. They pushed a heavily favored Atlanta Hawks team to a seven-game playoff series, even without their big man. A late-season injury forced Bogut to miss the playoffs.

The 2009–10 Bucks showed they were in good hands under Skiles and Hammond. Fears of a return to the dark days of the 1990s faded. Milwaukee, still without the injured Redd, did not play as well in 2010–11 as it had the previous season. Nevertheless, there were reasons for optimism for the fans, who embraced the team's rallying cry of "Fear the Deer!"

TIMELINE

1968
On January 22, the NBA awards an expansion franchise to a Milwaukee investment group headed by Marvin Fishman and Wesley Pavalon. The Bucks play their first game on October 16 and lose to the Chicago Bulls 89–84 in front of 8,467 at the Milwaukee Arena.

1969
A day that rivals any in Bucks history arrives March 19 when the team participates in a coin flip with the Phoenix Suns for the first pick in the 1969 NBA Draft. The stakes are the league rights to UCLA superstar center Lew Alcindor, and the Bucks win the flip.

1971
An NBA championship comes to Milwaukee on April 30 as the Bucks complete a four-game sweep of the Baltimore Bullets. Alcindor is named MVP of the regular season and the NBA Finals. He takes the name Kareem Abdul-Jabbar before the 1971–72 season.

1974
Oscar Robertson's retirement on September 3 follows Milwaukee's grueling seven-game loss to the Boston Celtics in the 1974 NBA Finals.

1975
Unhappy in Milwaukee, Abdul-Jabbar is traded to the Los Angeles Lakers on June 16. The Bucks receive center Elmore Smith, guard Brian Winters, forward David Meyers, and guard/forward Junior Bridgeman for Abdul-Jabbar and center Walt Wesley.

1983
Star guard Sidney Moncrief wins the first-ever NBA Defensive Player of the Year Award.

1985
Herb Kohl buys the Bucks from Jim Fitzgerald on March 1.

1986	The Bucks finish the 1985–86 regular season with a 57–25 record to win a seventh straight division title.
1987	Milwaukee goes 50–32 and places third in the Central Division. The Bucks fall in seven games to the Celtics in the Eastern Conference semifinals. Don Nelson resigns as Milwaukee's coach and vice president of basketball operations on May 27.
1988	The $91 million Bradley Center becomes the Bucks' home on October 1.
2001	The Bucks earn their first division title in 15 years by finishing the 2000–01 season with a 52–30 record.
2005	Andrew Bogut, a 7-foot center from Australia and the University of Utah, arrives with the first overall draft pick on June 28.
2006	Guard Michael Redd scores a team-record 57 points on November 11 against the visiting Utah Jazz. The Bucks lose 113–111.
2008	On April 11, John Hammond is named general manager. He introduces Scott Skiles as head coach on April 21.
2009	The Bucks take Brandon Jennings with the 10th pick in the 2009 NBA Draft on June 25. In his seventh game, on November 14, he scores 55 points in Milwaukee's 129–125 victory over the visiting Golden State Warriors, coached by Nelson.

QUICK STATS

FRANCHISE HISTORY

1968–

NBA FINALS
(1968– ; win in bold)

1971, 1974

DIVISION/CONFERENCE FINALS

1970, 1971, 1972, 1974, 1983, 1984, 1986, 2001

KEY PLAYERS
(position[s]; years with team)

Kareem Abdul-Jabbar (C; 1969–75)
Ray Allen (G; 1996–2003)
Andrew Bogut (C; 2005–)
Junior Bridgeman (F/G; 1975–84, 1987)
Terry Cummings (F; 1984–89, 1995–96)
Bob Dandridge (F; 1969–77, 1981–82)
Brandon Jennings (G; 2009–)
Marques Johnson (F/G; 1977–84)
Bob Lanier (C; 1980–84)
Jon McGlocklin (G; 1968–76)
Sidney Moncrief (G; 1979–89)
Michael Redd (G; 2000–)
Oscar Robertson (G; 1970–74)
Glenn Robinson (F; 1994–2002)
Jack Sikma (C/F; 1986–91)

KEY COACHES

Larry Costello (1968–77):
   410–264; 37–23 (postseason)
Don Nelson (1976–87):
   540–344; 42–46 (postseason)
George Karl (1998–2003):
   205–173; 14–18 (postseason)

HOME ARENAS

Milwaukee Arena (1968–87)
   Known as MECCA Arena
   (1974–87)
Bradley Center (1988–)

* All statistics through 2010–11 season

QUOTES AND ANECDOTES

The 1970–71 NBA champion Bucks fit the description of the team's nickname, as Kareem Abdul-Jabbar described them: "We didn't have bruiser guys; I certainly wasn't a bruiser. Look at the picture of me and Wilt [Chamberlain], and I'm the skinny guy in all these photos. I also was the fastest guy out there at my position. We used our speed to great advantage. Our front line was probably the fastest, with Greg Smith and Bobby Dandridge, and Oscar [Robertson] knew how to orchestrate the offense and exploit that. Oscar's basketball IQ, he was like Einstein."

Kareem Abdul-Jabbar said of the skyhook: "I don't recall it ever being blocked by someone who was guarding me. Maybe a few people got to it, coming to help where I couldn't see them. But if I knew where someone was, that person was not going to block that shot."

Sidney Moncrief's leaping ability was captured on a *Sports Illustrated* cover on February 13, 1978, while he was soaring to a two-handed dunk as a University of Arkansas Razorback. The Bucks featured him wearing a Superman costume on the cover of their 1984–85 media guide. Moncrief had a knee problem that he was told would limit his NBA career to about two years. The five-time All-Star played 11 seasons.

In the 2009–10 season, the Bucks had a huge international flavor to their frontcourt. At center were Andrew Bogut of Australia, and Dan Gadzuric and Francisco Elson, both of the Netherlands. At forward were Primoz Brezec of Slovenia, Carlos Delfino of Argentina, Ersan Ilyasova of Turkey, and Luc Richard Mbah a Moute of Cameroon. The team also had guard Roko Ukic of Croatia.

GLOSSARY

acquire

To add a player, usually through the draft, free agency, or a trade.

assist

A pass that leads directly to a made basket.

broadcaster

An announcer who describes or talks about sporting events on television or radio.

draft

A system used by professional sports leagues to select new players in order to spread incoming talent among all teams. The NBA Draft is held each June.

expansion

In sports, the addition of a franchise or franchises to a league.

free agent

A player whose contract has expired and who is able to sign with a team of his choice.

goaltending

Interfering with the flight of the ball near the basket.

inaugural

The first time something occurs.

postseason

The games in which the best teams play after the regular-season schedule has been completed.

realignment

A change in how teams are grouped.

rebound

To secure the basketball after a missed shot.

rival

An opponent that brings out great emotion in a team, its fans, and its players.

trade

A move in which a player or players are sent from one team to another.

FOR MORE INFORMATION

Further Reading

Abdul-Jabbar, Kareem, and Peter Knobler. *Giant Steps*. New York: Bantam Books, 1987.

Doucette, Eddie. *The Milwaukee Bucks and the Remarkable Abdul-Jabbar*. Englewood Cliffs, NJ: Prentice-Hall, Inc., 1974.

Pepe, Phil. *Stand Tall, the Lew Alcindor Story*. New York: Grosset & Dunlap, 1970.

Web Links

To learn more about the Milwaukee Bucks, visit ABDO Publishing Company online at **www.abdopublishing.com**. Web sites about the Bucks are featured on our Book Links page. These links are routinely monitored and updated to provide the most current information available.

Places to Visit

Bradley Center
1001 North Fourth Street
Milwaukee, WI 53203
414-227-0400
www.bradleycenter.com
This is the Bucks' home arena. The team plays 41 regular-season games here each season.

Kohl Center
601 West Dayton Street
Madison, WI 53715
608-263-5645
www.uwbadgers.com/facilities/kohl-center.html
This is the home arena of the University of Wisconsin men's and women's basketball teams. It is located on the school's campus in Madison.

Naismith Memorial Basketball Hall of Fame
1000 West Columbus Avenue
Springfield, MA
413-781-6500
www.hoophall.com
This hall of fame and museum highlights the greatest players in the history of basketball. Former Bucks players Kareem Abdul-Jabbar, Oscar Robertson, and Bob Lanier have been inducted here.

INDEX

About the Author

Gary Derong is a newspaper copy editor based in St. Paul, Minnesota. He is a native of Milwaukee, Wisconsin, who has followed the Bucks since their inception. Derong formerly was a sportswriter, columnist, and editor in Duluth, Minnesota. He lives with his wife and son.